LISTENING TO THE DARK

To Jean & Michael

Love & best
wishes

Peter x

By the same author

Not Cawed Fireweed Fa Now't *(2010) ShoeString press*

Thumbing from Lipik to Pakrac New and Selected *(2009) Waterloo Press*

Tony Bevan and Peter Street at The Turnpike Gallery *(2006)*

Trees Will Be Trees *(2001) Shoestring Press*

Still Standing *(1997) TowPath Press*

Out Of The Fire *(1993) Spike Books*

Acknowledgments 2011

Twelve poem sequence - Not Calwd Fireweed Fa Nowt: Shoestring press
ISBN: 978-907356 14 8
Tony Bevans paintings Turpike Gallery ISBN 0 9529470 99
VeloVision – Cycle Magazine
Lancashire Life
The Inquirer Unitarian newspaper
The Recusant (website)
Disability Arts online
Bolton Evening News
2River: Missouri U.S.A.
The Crazy OIK

Art work by Kate Houghton

Peter is a recipient of a Royal Literary Fund Grant and member of the Society of Authors

LISTENING TO THE DARK

Peter Street

for all my grandchildren

PENNILESS PRESS PUBLICATIONS

www.pennilesspress.co.uk

Published by

Penniless Press Publications 2012

ISBN 978-1-4717-6977-1

Front Cover: Peter and his mother – 1952
Back Cover: Peter and his mother 1998

CONTENTS

INTRODUCTION

His life story is that of an itinerant autodidact, with shades of The Ragged Trousered Philanthropists and Thomas Hardy's Jude. But Peter Street has defied decades of hardship and disability to become a war poet and BBC writer-in-residence, with four volumes of verse to his name.

Street, 59, is about to release his fifth volume after winning a grant from the Royal Literary Fund, the benevolent society set up to help professional writers in straitened times. Past beneficiaries have included Samuel Taylor Coleridge, DH Lawrence and James Joyce. "Poetry is usually written by people who are quite intelligent and come from good backgrounds, so I was cutting through all that," Street says.

Born in Wigan in 1948, the illegitimate son of a cotton millworker and an Irish-Spanish glassworker, Street was raised by his mother and a stepfather who offered her what Street describes as a "bizarre deal", whereby she gained the roof over her head in return for performing his household chores.

At school, Street struggled to spell or do basic sums, and it was clear he had a learning difficulty (it was eventually diagnosed as dyscalculia only five years ago). When he left at 15, with no qualifications and emerging epilepsy, he embarked on an employment odyssey, trawling for work from Cumbria to Kent, and doing jobs that included gravedigger, exhumer, slaughterhouse worker, baker, gardener, hotel porter and tree surgeon.

While in this last job, in 1982, he fell off a wagon and sustained a spinal injury that disabled him for life, but ultimately led to his reinvention as a poet. Recovering in hospital, he befriended an English literature teacher who inspired him to learn to read and to channel his extraordinary experiences into writing.

After belatedly failing his English O-levels, he finally found his voice when a Liverpool University lecturer offered him free tuition after noticing his potential through a charity that Street had founded for aspiring artists with disabilities. Since then, he's led a rollercoaster literary life - as war poet on a humanitarian convoy through Croatia in 1993, writer-in-residence for BBC Greater Manchester Radio, and co-architect of a 1998 Poetry Society project to take performance poetry into fish and chip shops in his beloved Wigan.

So what does he think of the hand destiny dealt him in the end? "Breaking my neck was one of the greatest things ever to happen to me," he says, with a chuckle. "I have been able to take time out from society and learn how to become a poet. I've had a fascinating life. It's been amazing."

James Morrison
The Guardian, Wednesday 17 December 2008

PLACES ON LOAN

Iceland

to W.H. Auden

Six minutes to landing
the other side of your letter to Byron
where you ask Louis
what he thought of Reykjavik

Your book is down
marked   then jammed
between belly and seat belt

glance to my left I see lunar
with clumps of bright coloured
corrugated houses that sort

of scrape on the teeth
and there's no trees
no trees which for me

an ex forester feels like I have
flown onto a planet where
there's been an end
or beginning of something

Rainbow Sculpture: Keflavik Airport

for all rainbows

Takes your breath away
this chunk of a rainbow
jagged eighty feet

up from the ground
in a car park
between two old bangers

no breaks between the colours
not even cracks
or rips with rain pockets

just a smooth chunk of rainbow
all the colours intact
for us to dip our fingers into.

First Taste Of Iceland

for mum

The air is so clean I want to eat it;
fill up on it the kind my mother
as a child first tasted on the Cork coast
the wind she'd say would rock her to sleep

Now it's my turn to live and experience
a dream   we stop the car
step out onto a white road
slicing two volcanic plains in half

where the earth is trying its best to froth over
disguise anything that even looks lunar
and I filled my belly just like I did
with her Sunday dinner.

Hallgrim's Church, Reykjavik

for everyone with Dyspraxia and Dyscaculia

That church from
where I'm standing:
here bottom of the hill
between green
and yellow houses

south side of Reykjavik
I'm sure is the space-ship
Miss Clarkson let me draw

in her 1959 maths class
while other kids were busy
working on fractions.

It has a stair case
on the outside like the one
I pretended to climb
sit close my eyes

and wait for the count down

Café Rosenberg, Reykjavik

Playing dominoes
in a Rosenberg corner
other side of the bar

from a blues band
getting ready to kill us
with: "For Your Love"
when a woman

with white hair running
all the way down
to her early eighties

slapped us with a 'double nine'

then recited a poem
about the friday night
she first made love

to her flight bomber boyfriend
in a cold February corn field

the night before Dresden………

Blue Lagoon Spa In Lunar Iceland

An inch of blue
from a rainbow
just plopped out

splashing down
this side of Keflavik airport
a few million years
before the U.S.

landed bomber planes
where he practised his
"One giant leap for mankind"

their silliness long gone
I am with my grandchildren
wriggling our toes

in that very same plop of rainbow
thinking this is the closest
I will ever get to the moon.

Glaumbaers (Icelandic Grass Roofs)

for all Sacred Places

Grass covered roofs
like our Anderson shelter
dad was clipping

the October of '57
when me and Kathleen
decided to hide

out the way of "Sputnik 1"
after grown ups in butchers
and paper shops promised

there would be severe flooding
and things dropping out of the sky.

Dancing Sculptures: Perlan, Reykjavik

Take it easy
you can stop showing off
yes   it's good to see you too
sorry for being so long

I've been listening to the dark
grudging about the day light
being so long   too well liked
a bully   having its own way

even trying the discrimination card

until I said another few weeks
boot will be on the other foot
then we'll see who's complaining.

Hearts and Minds - (*Lupinus nootkatensis*)

for all Legumes

Regiments   blue
sometimes white

are ready to take over
a lunar part of Iceland
determined to stay

moon like where its soaked
salted and blown
every try into the sea

desperation now turns
to Lupins their rocket-heads
ready for action

leaves shape of the hand
open   wanting to shake
and let their nitrogen roots

alive the soil in a new
beginning   yes   come on
let's hear it for the Lupins.

My North West

Bolton

Tongue Cemetery

for all gravediggers

My first chit
with "pauper" written
in red ink across

a smaller than normal
piece of paper with
no lines and nothing
to fill in   blank

except for "Alex"

Photograph of '63

for Albert Lomax

Eleven of us Bolton Boys team,
lined up on Bromwich Street,
on the very spot our heroes,
Lofthouse, Hopkinson

Freddy Hill had stood. Now
some one wants us to say cheese
we stand with our backs
to the big house

which saw Charlton,
Duncan Edwards, Puskas
and Pele in warm-ups
for something bigger

still friends: they stood here
right here where we stand
shoulder to shoulder
like cut-out paper figures

waiting to be stretched.

Blue Lagoon: Belmont

Green pastures scramble
downhill stopping inches
from the waters edge

trees already there
wave their arms
trying to warn kids

away from a black jetty
over the reservoir with
a bad reputation for taking

anyone especially young boys
who jump in for the fun of it
a dare   a kiss   a first fumble

what-ever innocence
makes no difference
not with this baby

where miles below
compassions are frozen
shackled to all those lost kids

just sitting there arms folded
waiting in a long   long-line
for something to happen.

Rivington Unitarian Chapel

Shrubs on the outside wall
are clambering up on fingertips
to leaded windows

after yew tree at the front gate
asked them to take
one peep to see

if a tall pulpit is still there
against a wall relaxed
welcoming everyone

with bible stories poetry
the odd joke or two
and check if those box pews

from three hundred years
before were still sitting there
or had moved

stretched gone walkabout
when whispers start
to leap-frog over the

front few grave stones
back to yew tree saying:
"Everything is has always."

Aliens

Dusk   me and mum
short-cut through
Belmont Dye Works
when a light from a building

pushes four men
with green heads
out of the main block
into their tea-break

for one moment
half-a-breath-even
aliens have landed
north of Bolton

sharing fags
and drinking tea
from tin mugs.

Hotel Room

for all Night Porters

Party girl remembering
her friend she found dead
in a Bolton bathroom

after a night out   pissed
and pissed again trying
with every breath and breath

of her body and soul
to stop her going
but couldn't

one year on it's the turn
of her young apprentice
his first office party
to be pissed and pissed again

slumped over a shower basin
face flat against anti-slip ribs
where hundreds of customers

have stood washing whatever
down a plug hole
his stomach lining
stuck to his face

she sobers up stacks her tears
behind her   takes control
puts him on his back
and breathes and breathes

him back to life.

Another Sideline – 1957 Bolton

for Thomas Edgar Street

Two shillings
for every dead dog or cat
run over   poisoned even shot

would be waiting with heads on
heads off   maybe other bits
missing   every time

my nine years entered
his fire-hole where sulphur
smacked me in the nose

Dad would clang open
an incinerator door   turn
pick up Rover or Tabby

he kept separate from the coal

with a clean cloth
he would first wipe off
any dirt or blood

then giving them a last stroke
he'd throw them in
and I would watch

someone's pet melt into nothing.

Bolton Lion Tamer – January 1897

for all circus animals

In Gladiator gear
he taunted Tyrant the African Lion
who a few months before

had already snacked
on the young tamers arm
spit out the sword hand
needing more salt

Maccarte chest out   boasted
to crowds he was boss
of all lions   until Tyrant
leapt and ripped the tamers

scalp off in one

now with a taste of things to come
the lion became boss
and made a right meal
of Thomas Maccarte

Maths With Everything – 1957/58

for everyone on the spectrum

With my very best head
I tried   really tried to add
even multiply none
of it worked

the numbers did their best
to understand me it just
wouldn't.

So Mam in her biscuit moments
cut out shapes numbers
nought to twenty
I was eating sums   sums

after bacon and eggs
finney haddock or colcannon
streaming best butter

none of it worked
not even when teacher
hit my head   side on

with the board duster
to "Knock some sense in"
I tried to number the tears

but lost count.

Mates of '58

That outside toilet where mam
used to traipse our night time
piss-pots before work

is now redundant after
a posh inside one ganged up
with sink and bath

to take over our spare bedroom

it's now a short walk to my
rainy day place I share
with the old toilet bowl

retired   bored   does nothing
except sit there reading strips
of Bolton Evening News

stringed on that side of the wooden door

where a paraffin lamp
surrounded by parched strands
of whitewash lights up

my marble assault course
with all the cracks dips
and holes in those stone flags

which lifted me and my glass friends
to marble champion of Blackburn Road

Moss Bank Way

for Fred Thompson

1920
breaking his arm on
a Durham farm where
he was born and bred

his dad sort of fixed it
on the kitchen table with
herbs and half a dozen

gobs of home made cider
knocking Fred out while his
arm was guessed back into place

boasting never cried once
even though he could never
straighten it again

1972
Heading home
after four days of laying
field drains   a cow

in trauma feet away
from cars and people
no second thoughts

Fred fumbled his dentures

into a used handkerchief
stripped down   half naked
he handed me the calves feet

in my own world
waiting for his nod

I held tight to those

few inches of life.

He was pushing mum
back up into a birthing position
"Get your shirt off man
and pull   you lazy bugger

pull slide your hands inside"
we balanced somewhere
between life and death
my hands and brain lost

while Fred digging his heels
deeper into blood and manure
rhythmed "Heave one – two – three

heave pull you lazy bastard pull"
We lost both calf and mother
flaking black twist he filled

tamped his pipe tears streamed
a face you could strop a razor on.

Moor Lane Bus Station

for everyone with Dyspraxia and Dyscalculia

I'm lost on a bus station
in the middle of everywhere
lost between numbers and places
known or unknown

lost between all left
and right turns until
the woman at Information

surrounded with time tables
leaned against the back wall
she hands me a map
I can't understand

"Can you please tell me
where and what bus number?"
She thinks I'm winding her up

and shouts "next please"

Howe Bridge (Atherton) Bandstand

for Andy Bubble

A stroll into woods
on a path floodlit
with buttercups and dandelions

past a gang of nettles
lolling about on the corner.
A push through layers of tunes

from last Summer's brass bands

clinging to your mind
pulling you down into the woods
deeper

towards the young sycamores
gathered around the wooden
bandstand built by someone

who thought his New Jerusalem
is there among the trees.

Howe Bridge (Atherton) Summer Night

for Tyldesley Brass Band

Somewhere between
Blue Sombrero and Love
Is A Many Splendored Thing

Summer trees gathered behind us
while some ferns   shy   peeped
from behind a young oak

swaying   beckoning the rest
of Briar Woods summer flora
and fauna to join in

they did whole families
of nettles docks hazels
alders and sycamores surrounded us

joined by a few thousand insects
camouflaged crept up
safe   they settled

underneath our chairs
between bottles of wine
while enjoying a bit of brass.

Mums Funeral: Howe Bridge Cemetery, 1998

My hand   a mind of its own
took over – back to being
the good Catholic I crossed myself:

"In the Name of The Father,
The Son and The Hoy Ghost,
Amen"

Stepping onto a wooden staging
back to being the gravedigger
I threaded ropes
through those brass rings

then lifting her onto
six foot of forever
I lowered her slower
than slow down

into her Heaven.

Nell Lane, Manchester, 1983)

for Tony Bevan

I have been re-born
here on this tarmac road
where I have landed
neck broken

everything tingling   burning
my legs and my body
have gone walk-about

I want them back
no   this is not a sick joke
tell everyone to look for them

my neck is broken

please do not turn away
I am the same me
ok I may look different

still me   honest

for the Tony Bevan/Peter Street exhibition: Turnpike Gallery, Leigh

Pain Relief

never walked a red road
one of those things you don't do
not the norm
I am walking one with my nurse

love my nurse
and her morphine
wow with the tequila
my friends brought in

this is more than a sunrise
my pain has been swallowed
and I have gaps in my head
holes as big as windows

fancy windows
with rafters
I have rafters in my head
wow

First commissioned/published for the Tony Bevan/Peter Street exhibition: Turnpike Gallery, Leigh

Escapees

for all spinal injuries

Spinal Ward B   remember
I am the one who got you into
Astral Projection
and we ghosted out of the ward

to the nearest chip shop
bringing back new spinal cords
for everyone   yes me
the one who took the piss

out of that neck prop
do you still look up
when they are washing your bollocks
and go all red   I bet you do

First commissioned/published for the Tony Bevan/Peter Street exhibition: Turnpike Gallery, Leigh

Pavements: Back into the Out

for every wheelchair user

They've pushed me out
into a Gulliver world
everything's changed
streets, café's toilets

and it's raining   pavements wet
my first day in the big outside
this is it   no more practice

hard   hands burning
arms hanging off
I move to and fro
lines criss-crossing

all over the place
trying to dodge dog shit

First commissioned/published for the Tony Bevan/Peter Street exhibition: Turnpike Gallery, Leigh

Lipik, Croatia 1993 (*Red Corridor)*

for the Little Hulton Police Convoy team

moments when young screams
dodging Bosnian shells paint
a corridor red

red as red
they run towards
the cellar of their orphanage
lights knocked out

dark in minutes   their pain
behind them solidifying
over the walls and stanchions

months later it's all been
hosed down scrubbed clean
of all screams and tears

spotless until I tread
on a tiny bubble of memory
explodes for all of us to see

First commissioned/published for the Tony Bevan/Peter Street exhibition: Turnpike Gallery, Leigh

Tony Bevan's Table Top

The importance of this
is harder than you think

it was about being young
with no understanding
of who or where I came from

just saying I was a table
got me into all sorts of trouble
but it's ok now

it was the politics
of which came first
the chair or the table?
got to me

of course the tables came first

the chairs came seated
themselves around us
see what was going on
look important

besides what else is a chair
good for? they can't
sit up straight and when
have you heard of anyone

Breaking Bread on a chair?
so I thought I'd celebrate
and put my best top on

do you like it ?

Waiting Rooms

- for Anne Peaker

Nine metal chairs
fifty-five-and-a-half floor tiles,
black spot on the wall

I glare at, closing my right eye
then left   shifting it from side to side
up and down a kiddie's game

while other people bury their eyes
in magazines
first the Agony Aunt
then a half-completed crossword

the cream cake on the recipe page
helps me forget where I am

In The Citizens Advice Bureau

for Kelly

A young volunteer
sits on her chair   spine erect
I want to stroke kiss hold
each bubble of her vertebrae
straight   a spirit level   perfect

unlike mine   curved with
twenty-odd fractures of osteoporosis

my eyes want that shoulder strap
to fall again   to feel her
filling the room

she   innocent of all this
slowly fingers pages
looking for an answer to my problem

Halliwell Road Bike Shop

for Michael Warren

Falcon bike
finger thin wheels
with five Olympic rings

on its yellow and black frame
"Derailleur" gears
and drop handle bars

I'm telling you
teased us from the back wall
of Kays Bike shop

by hanging just inches above
all the money
we had in the world

Iron Master (Sculpture by David Kemp)

for all 6,000 employees of Consett Steelworks

Two human looking aliens
just rose twenty feet or so
in front of me

pushed up through ground
trod solid with clogs
and hob-nailed boots

giants dressed in iron bits
fallen from all those
men and women

whose sweat   tears
breaths and bodies
had fallen where I was standing

there in the middle
of a now Durham cycle route

Starting Again

for all cyclist

Maybe its about right
stopping the clocks
give us time   time
to take breath

help us start again
round the steam engine time
or better still push-bikes

yes each family could be given
a daily dose of push-bike
killing our gridlock disease

in months   days even

a world without knuckles
and blood pressures
all over our steering wheels

yes   lets hear it for the push-bike

Wheelbarrow

Point me in the direction
you are going before loading
here are my arms grab hold

you shouldn't be the one sweating

lift   I'll pull you along
I'm here to help   any weight
should be on my shoulders
where I'm strongest

No listen   you are doing it wrong
Yes I'm only a wheelbarrow
with no other ambitions
except to help

make the work easier   quicker
honest   nothing more than that
I don't want or need anything
from you   honest

Radio Alarm Clock

Dying   we checked everything:
plug   loose wires
scoured the internet

for radio alarm fixers

anyone   not bothered
about names or titles
just as long as we

don't lose it to some
recycling mountain

all our married life
it's been with us
even on some holidays

forty years never once
complained   stopped
not even a protest

it's now retired on a shelf
in my office facing
a window with easy views

Bread

for Café Med' Platt Bridge

A slight tug
rip of freshly baked bread
and the warm way
it fills your nose

pulls all the juices
down
from the roof of your mouth
ready to taste
even before it's there

an anticipation
of something so simple
as breaking bread
for all of us

is what we want to do
again and again
before we die

Flora and Fauna

WE THE PROPRIETORS WANT OUR WORLD BACK

EXTRAORDINARY MEMBERS MEETING:
AGENDA: COUNCIL OF WAR:

Copperas Lane, Haigh Hall, Wigan

"Plant geneticists are finding that plants can communicate with each other as well as with insects by coded gas exhalations"

James Donahue – Living Universe

Rumex

Dock leaves *Rumex obtusifolius*

Dozens of docks
making their way down
through fields
to a meeting place

in the front meadow. Stop
wave and cheer

buttercups and hemlocks
leading lines of wild flowers
down Copperas Lane

towards Haigh Hall
where regiments
of dandelion seeds
are parachuting in……

Taraxacum

First To Speak

for all dandelions (*Taraxacum officinale*)

I am a dandelion

Yes, one of those who feel
we have more to offer
than this tarmac they like
so much.

It’s why I’m here
to see about a peace deal,
compromise,
their last chance – so to say

before it gets really serious.
Ok, mistakes have been
on both sides, but while

they are trying to kill us all …..

well, it’s like this:
we are a big family
with lots of friends

who are also losing patience.
This is their last chance

Urtica

Open Floor

for All Stinging Nettles Urtica dioica

Honest we have tried
our very best to keep out
of their way

we know and respect
how much they like to be in charge
At first we tried hiding
behind old farm machinery

then it was round the back
of rundown sheds
and in dark corners
but it somehow

never quite seemed enough

So we thought it might
now this is only a suggestion
might be worth getting together

call it a new beginning
with dock leaf as a go between.
What do you think?

Buttercups *Ranunculus acris*

Agitators.

No Playtime is over.
It's finally come down
to giving them a taste

of who we really are

their sheep and cattle
took notice when we first
burned their tongues
not forgetting their stomachs

they now leave us alone

No it's gone way past
anything called reasonable
we need to act now before
they destroy us all

so who will second this motion

for all of our roots
from all of our families
to creep out of sight

just below the
surface of this world
and take over?

Plantago

Plantain *Plantago Major*

Mediator

Please, listen before you go
getting here has taken
millions of years -
we cannot throw that away.

This is not who we are,
we are the chosen ones
healers – not warmongers

you must say no to this motion.

Confusion is getting around
some of the grasses
are sharpening their blades

the hemlocks are being loaded
with more and more poisons
this is getting out of hand

please don't second this motion
we are better than this

let's give them one last chance

Bellis

Wishful Thinkers

Daisies *(Bellis Perennis)*

for all lawn daisies

We will stand up
and be counted   yes
all the daisies in all the world
are making their way here

crowding the lawn
side of Banks Street Chapel
before going on to Haigh Hall

where in our hundreds -
maybe thousands we will say
no to war. If Bolton is difficult

then where ever you are
stand up and be counted
say no to this madness

Convolvulus

Assassins *Convolvulus arvensis*

field bindweed

You buttercups are all the same
we know you hate
all two hundred and fifty
of our family.

Jealous are we

no one would suspect
who we are and what we do
it's our beauty you know

from being in the lanes
relaxed frightened of no one
this goads you doesn't it

having to ask us for help

we want to hear it
come on admit –
you cannot do what we do

what we have always done

your dirty work in choking
the slow death out of all those
you despise because they are
respected

so   who is it this time
daises   dandelion   streams
fences who or what

Symphytum

Comfrey (nip-bone) *Symphytum officinale*),

Aye many a time
bandaged myself
around their broken bones

after clog or bare knuckle
fighting all for the prize
of a crust

no myself and my family
are menders of hurt
we do not do war

maybe yourselves need
some bandaging
why don't you come

and see us sometime
we are always here
there's no charge

Centaurea cyanus

Cornflower *Centaurea cyanus*

for Sue Bell

We gave them blue
as much as they wanted
with no contracts free for ever

then in a wisdom we didn't understand
they tried to poison or burn us out

but going to war is not who
we are   maybe it's about
starting again another go

would showing them
a world without colour help

we could get friends round
for a fancy knees up
with no colour   no fun

that's how it would be

no for us cornflowers
war is never an option

Fallopia japonica

Japanese knotweed *Fallopia japonica*

No colours no fancy knees up
you'll have us all crying
we're talking big boys
stuff now

it's higher in the scheme
of everything this is what we do
it's us or them

they have been here
in a flicker of time
and already trying

their best to destroy themselves
and us   no   this is survival
so let's help them on their way

see we can be generous
and yes
we are going to war

Digitalis

Foxglove *Digitalis purpurea*

Hello is anyone listening

Yes   I'm a volunteer steward
on this my first conference
so can you all please calm down

and tell me how else

to get your attention
and yes, I'm sorry
if ringing my bells
nearly burst your eardrums

but how else am I going to get you
all heading down Copperas Lane
in single file
behind the hemlocks?

Epilobium

Rosebay willowherb (Pioneer species) *Epilobium angustifolium*

Carry on kid bout time
wi had sum yung blood

at these things

bells don't bother us
in fact nowt at all
bothers us willow herb

bar snotty noses
down in that Haigh Hall
meadow wonting war

wiv sin it dun it
survivd it weer not calld
fireweed fa nowt ya know

wars got us noweer
wots lackin here
is sum common sense

down theer fa dancin
up here fa thinkin
war indeed

they wont their arses kickin'
weer off wam
is anyone cumin?

Invasion

Warning – This Is Not A Practise

Icebergs – Are Melting Towards Us

Here   Now   Prepare

Sand Sedge Carex arenaria

Like all families we have fought

for all our sakes
that is now behind us
there's an army washing towards us

waves of them
from their land of ice and water
a taster they're calling it

we have to be ready –
otherwise we will all
be washed away

none of us will survive.
This where our fight really starts
come and stand with us

here next to my triangular stems
shields against their salt-burn
we have to slow those waves down

take the battle to them   here
on these dunes,
so all of you listen,

Sand Sedges are natural warriors
we take root,   colonise,   safe in numbers
know what we have to do

are you with us ?

Soft Field Rushes *Juncus effuses*

Aye weel join ya
we're not mard
water doesn't bother us
in fact nowt does

that's why sum think
weer a push oer
all because we like ta stand
feet in water enjoyin

the family craice
wats rong wi that
I tell ya it teks a lot
ta get us gooin but wen we do

get out o' ta road
ask those Alien things
dressed in them black plastic bales
who landed in nearly every farmers field

thinking they would fritten us
into submission aye til
wi started explodin
then wid freeze frame

thousands of us
just like cluster bombs
fritten us
aye fritten us my arse

Sweet flag *Acorus calamus*
Kusanagi-no-Tsurugi ("Grass Cutting Sword").

Yes we are with you

You wanted warriors
with sharp sword leaves
who can slice through
what ever those waves

will bring   well that is us

you are forgetting
it is here   now
just ask Japan

and we see grasses from India

even America   when the time comes
we will wave our flag leaves
give those waves

chance to surrender

Nile Grass *Acroceras Macrum*

Blackpool Tower callin
there's sum grass up ere
lost lad says he's from Africa
somethin bout the sea

teckin back the land
I don't think lads
much English says he's
directin operations

that's war time stuff
wot's gooin on –
then he tries tellin me
Nile grasses luv water

and we haven't ta worry
their grasses can produce
all the hay we wont
wot's gooin on and

how cum a lad from Africa
is five undred feet
nearer ta clouds
directin operations

here on top ot tower

floodins Africa
I blame it on them birds
bloody nuisance at times

Common Bent Grass *Agrostis capillaries*

Eh mind who you're
calling common
we've dressed some
of the best golf courses

in the world   mind you
I suppose when comes down to it
we've all a bit of common
in us even those fancy pants

Presidents Kings and Queens
whose trod all over me

but we'll all look the same
when those waters come
to flood us all away
time and tide kid

time and tide

Bamboo

Bet that sticks in your throat
wanting our help
to hold back the floods
how many years

since you last called us
bad- boys   even bullies?

If we wanted the world
would be ours   what's the point
we like relaxed   friends
loads of friends like

Pandas and let locals
use us for houses and boats
it's all about sharing

it's what we do

when the waters come
and they will
just give us a shout
we'll see what we can do

Sea Arrow Grass *Triglochin maritime*

Salt doesn't bother us

Well one of us has to like it
because there is burn
in those waters

joking apart

those sand sedges are right
we haven't much time
even from here

on the edge of the shoreline
we can feel it   yes
here on the marshes

its on its way

waves and waves
are on their way
we have to colonise

yes, we could take over
but not now we have got
to be as one

this is our one chance
to show who we really are
yes we are grasses

but not something to be walked
over not any more

Couch Grass *Elytrigia repens*

What's the panic

waves flooding
its just a joke
we are the invaders

who can keep underground
out of harms way doing
our own thing and rhizoming

its what we do listen

forget all the propaganda
of icebergs global warming
just tripe

like always we stay strong

problem there's no problem
alright if we are split we multiply
like I said no problem

its just water who cares

Sweet Vernal-grass *Anthoxanthum odoratum*

Eh   you just hold on a second
an invasion is imminent
ice cold water waves

towards us yet you

typical couch grasses
are again just looking out
for yourselves all

of us have to come together

if we took notice of you
who would look after
butterflies leaf hoppers

sun beetles grass bugs
and thousands of other workers
tell me that

that's why we at Sweet Vernal Grass
need to keep the pressure up
we have a workforce second to none

that's how we want to keep it

Ice Grass *Phippsia algida*

Yes this is the Arctic tundra
where else would it be?

Sorry bad day
the water keeps complaining
about it being cold
what does it expect

all day long moan moan
and more moan
is it me but this land

of ice and water is about
remote   real   cold
if it can't cope now well

that shocks us back to the war
we need a truce   maybe get the
usurpers to clean up their act

anyone talked to the Icebergs
about staying solid   after-all
it's in their best interest

Radical bracken ferns *Pteridium aquilinum*

wots up wi yor lot
a thowt this meetin
wus grown ups only

aw them millions o years
crawlin under erth
outa way

werz it getten ya
no weer   ya need
sumert else

ta breck ther conca
an divide its ow theyv
kept us unda

teck us   wi look awreet

easy onth eyes
but we av carcinogenic
up ar sleeves

wot av yo getten
nowt except yoor arm
tell ya wiv got ta rid arselves

ov thees new Charlies
hoo think thay own tha place
so iv yoov ad enof   ov them

then cum an join us
an tagetha weel beet um

BEETLES

Operation . --- . . - . --- - … . - - … . - .. . (Probable)

Haigh Hall Wigan

S.O.S.
… --- … Are there any
Assassin or Ambush Bugs out there

we are a company of Hawthorns
there are about hundred or so of us
and yes we are sharpening our thorns

but we alone cannot keep out
Asian Longhorn beetles
and their allies

we need more ground forces

… --- …

Calling all Checkered Beetles
there are battalions
of Long Horns here now

bore holes are everywhere
maples and birches
are lying dead

… --- …

2. Borsdane Woods – Westhoughton

Calling all Longhorns
and yes that means you

who are struggling on your own
day in day out
getting no where fast

those days are now behind us
we can be strong and do the job
we were put on this earth

to do   calling all Longhorns
yes   you before that trees pitch
comes out and glues you to the bark

this is your chance
to find out what really works
and where and how we can finally

dead them all

calling all Longhorns

take one minute out
remember those poor beetles
who tested the waters and teased

millions of elms into suicide
even then we were still ignored
THEY took no notice of the warning

Well here me beetles
where ever you are
our time has come

3. Calling All Longhorn Beetles

The New Forest, Hampshire, England

I am just an old oak
but you Wolf trees
with your multi stemmed branches

who for centuries have bullied
the light and strength
from other law abiding trees

yes, you who have dodge your way
out of every chainsaw
this is now about all of us

that's why with your experiences
it's time to step into the breach
and lead all the other trees

to safety we know you wolves

have survived such attacks
so please show us how to defeat
these Asian Longhorns Beetles

we need all the help you can give

4. Wolf King

Eh just a minute
we have good relations
with beetles especially the bark ones

and have done for centuries

they feel safe with us
we look after them
and in turn ….

well you know don't you
just ask any Clerid beetle
or even some of those fancy

coloured assassin bugs

who holiday on us Wolves
it's all about living together
and helping each other out

symbiosis is the future

***

Some of us Wolves have to be
head and shoulders
above the rest   it's what we

were born to do   keep an eye on
you lot especially after the great unbalance
THEY have created

It's the reason the Longhorns are
leading this attack thinking
they can wipe us all out

they think - but word is coming through

the Shrikes (Butcher birds)
are waiting in the wings

Lets hear it for the Shrikes

A wolf is a tree whose main stem is twisted and over-shoots/takes its neighbours

5. Fellow Beetles

Thank you,   for coming

Let me say I'm just an ordinary
bark beetle
much the same as you

and yes its taken us
hundred or so years of explaining
to those mighty trees

who we are   and how we don't
want to hurt anyone   we even talked
symbiosis   they laughed at us

they're not laughing now

This is why I called a meeting:
help from Those who destroy everything

THEY have created trees with resistant
strains – freaks to fight their battles
then rest on imagined victories

this my fellow beetles is just the beginning
it's our very survival we are apart of them
they apart of us

why can those trees not see this

like you I have heard rumours
reinforcements from the Americas

it is now more than that
more regiments of Asian Longhorns
and their allies

are on their way here   now

Fellow Beetles this is our chance
To destroy everything on this planet
We have the power

6. Clerid Beetles *Cleroidea*

Bluebell Woods, Bolton

Listen-up   this is a code one

So napkins on   its feast time
this is us   professionals
no emotion in doing the job

we were born to do   this is us

So be careful out there
those Longhorns are not fussy
who they take down

they'll do anything to save their larvae

the drill should now be second nature
just turn on your back
and play dead

yes the Longhorns are that stupid

so helmets on   remember
their bore tunnels can be dark
and tight   good luck stay safe

and fill up on those Asian Longhorn larvae

7. Wigan Shrikes *Lanius excubitor*

Two Shrikes to cover
all of Haigh Hall's
250 acre estate

proving once again we are
the best Butcher-birds
this side of Texas winning
every known prize

for the way we hang out our prey
experienced yes we are
two of us seems impossible
it's what we do and have done

here for fifty years or more

Asian Longhorns were never
on this estate at least not before
the Unbalancing and have you seen
those sails on Copperas Lane windmill

they're covered in Longhorns

we need your help this is more
important that us Strikes
it's about putting

our differences to one side
Jays Magpies Crows
We need your skills

this is our chance to prove
who we are and stop the wipe out.

8. **Magpies** *Pica pica*

Us magpies don't need
to prove anything

at least not to you Shrikes
we'll see who is who
when it all kicks off

and the blood-baths begins
there'll be no time to hang
those Longhorns up

in pretty neat patterns

this is going to get bloody that's
why I'm calling in the Crows
they'll come in from behind

in pairs doing what they do best
watch out for the Jays they'll be
sparking over the tops of

those beetles rocking and rolling
with their fine pincer movements
an army of decent soldiers

well we are not decent good or fair
Corvus are the stuff of nightmares

***

I'm an Haigh Hall magpie
telling you: our members
to listen to the Shrikes call
they are not misguided birds

yes, they are loners we cannot
hold that against them

they can be relied on
unlike humans who patronise
us with their silly rhyming games

and saluting us
what's all that about
not only but they've caused

this mess so why should we
step into the breach
we'd get no thanks.

9. Wipe Out   Shrikes

And you are supposed to be
the clever ones Aye
clever my bum

typical magpies
look after your little selves
you don't get it   do you

this is not about us and them
it's not even about territories
this is about us all

coming together as one
here in this windmill field
of Haigh Hall

where the Unbalancing ends
it has to do   we have to forget
individual   that was then

now   is in this field between windmill
and woods where the rebalancing
begins   look

for yourself   hoverflies bee   moles
even the foxgloves and their pollinators
are coming up the field

even they know it's right

10. Bumblebees *Bombus terrestris*

We took a day off
to listen to this rubbish
why are you blaming each other

for the trouble we are in
none of us have caused this
it's exactly what THEY want

us to think look at the way
you are squabbling
behind this windmill out of the way
as though you are ashamed

of being beetles or birds

trees or flowers no this is our chance
come together show who we are
what we can do collectively

that's why we Bumblebees
have voted for strike action
the world is going to have one summer

without us pollinators

before the damage has gone beyond repair
we have to prove the importance
of us and all our brother and sisters

for all our sake we cannot
let it happen together
we are strong stronger

than anything they can
muster up are you with us ?

11. Hoverflies *Syrphidae*

Yo   let's not get carried away here
this is getting too personal
too angry

listen   we wouldn't be here
but for our specific job
you are trying to think

like them   don't

symbiosis is the secret
Haigh Hall has
brought in chamomile

parsley   buckwheat and yarrow
to keep us busy   happy
plant to plant pollinating

its what we do

you all have to start
thinking like a field
that is the way forward

back to getting the balance right

12. Checkered Beetles *Cleridae Latreille*

the Hover flies are right
we have to get back
to the balance

we are not the problem
arguing among ourselves
will get us no where

this Haigh Hall field
is giving us the chance
to sort our difficulties out

we have to ask
was it the barrels of oil
who caused the problem

or was it the engines
are they prepared
to meet us here in this field

behind this windmill

do we tell them to sort
 themselves out
or we will do it for them

and with it will come hell

TREES AS ARTISTS

- for John Lucas

Trees as Artists

We are painters,
natural artists.
Each summer with long arms

using green or sometimes yellow. Just
happy to stand painting your streets,
gardens, roads.

We get fed up
with green, rub it out

But we are soon at it again:
golds, reds, bright yellows!

....

Pollarded Willows

Yes, our branches are clenched fist,
angry at you for clogging our leaves.

That's why our cousins the elms
started the rebellion.
You called it Dutch Elm Disease,
blaming the beetle.
It's always somebody else.

They cut off their own water supply
in protest.

It was suicide.

Oak To Lombardy Poplar

Why are you standing to attention?
Never stand to attention
for a car. OK, you're the new kid
on the block.

You only want to impress.
 Forget it.
They don't give a monkey's
about you.

They're bad news.
So just slow down,
it'll happen.
I know I'm an old fart
and, yes, you may
head-and-shoulder me.

But you've missed
the best times……..

Ranunculus (*Buttercups*)

Did you not see the signs
let me spell it out for you
Ranunculas only

saying that you made
all six hundred of our family
laugh by sending in

the sorrel
to try and sweeten us up
laugh   we've not laughed

so much since the tiny humans
tested us for butter
can you believe that

bright young and pretty
is all they see while
ignoring the real us

so take your single roots
to the other fields
stay with your own kind

Bluebells *Hyacinthoides non-scripta*

Ranunculus only you
are joking
we all need to let others in

being happy is what it's all about
look why don't you give it a go
join us in the woods

your yellow mingled in
with our blue talk about
a show stopper

like you we can run
underground take over
that's been tried and failed

besides who really wants to
do that no do you
and your six hundred a favour

be happy forget about
being alone join us
I know you'll love it

....

Atropa belladonna *deadly nightshade*

Yes   that's it go into the woods
have a play around
with the blues

look all pretty loved
every ones favourite
pretending is what it is
once you start that
they will all want
a piece of your field

keep your respect
stretch out those roots
take over

being bad is good
no one messes with you
mixing strengthens them

make the sign bigger
Ranunculus only
you have been warned

Horse Tail *Equisetum arvense* 25 Million Years ago

Talk about a bright light

my god everything just
fizzled right in front of us
even those flying Charlies

taking out our tops
thirty meters up
flopped and fizzled

gone

talk about goodnight vienna
no skin off our nose
they thought they owned the place

prancing about like they did

who ever switched on
that light did us a favour
our tops went meters

underground where no one
could get them

especially the new Charlies
who think they own the earth
not for very long

Ginkgo and the Mares Tail

forget being those Charlies
they're not forever
here   now is comfortable
easy

nothing pounding up behind us

it's good   They like us
we look after Them
what's so wrong in that

don't forget
you're not the size
you once were

when everything looked up to you

come on join us
and chill
you'll get more respect that way

Too Late *Neomarica caerulea*

respect that's a laugh

it's one thing we've never had
but now the floods are coming
you want our help

show you how to walk
escape from the icebergs

no it's too late
for all of that making friends
nice little chats

we are who we are
walking our way out
is what we do making our way out
of here you should have

listened have a nice drowning

The Beginning

for all grasses

Excuse me
why weren't grasses
informed about this take over

why should you
have all the fun
we are the obvious choice

and probably suffered
more than most

remember those Charlies
ripping us apart
regardless

No   they will not let us rest
there is only one way
yes we need to talk tactics

floods are on their way
did someone mention
about starting a fresh

is it not too late?